AF571048

I am unique

Kirsten Sar

MINDFUL AFFIRMATIONS FOR SPECIAL KIDS

I am unique

This is how special kids develop strong personalities

Kirsten Sar

FSC
www.fsc.org
MIX
Papier aus verantwortungsvollen Quellen
Paper from responsible sources
FSC® C105338

Production and publishing: BoD – Books on Demand, Norderstedt

Bibliographic information from the German National Library:

The German National Library lists this publication in the Deutsche Nationalbibliografie; detailed bibliographic data are available in the Internet at http://dnb.dnb.de.

Script: © 2023 Copyright by Kirsten Sar

Illustration: 2023 by Thejani (Anisha)

Webseite: kirstensar.com

ISBN: 9783757886059

I am unique and special, just the way I am.

I have the potential to achieve my goals and dreams.

My differences make me extraordinary and exceptional.

My voice and opinion matter and deserve to be heard.

I am loved, supported and encouraged by others.

I am strong and brave.
I can overcome any challenge.

I have unique talents and gifts that bring joy to others.

I am proud of myself. I am proud of my courage, my strength, the things I achieve and everything I do.

I am defined by my spirit and character.

I celebrate my achievements, big and small.

I love my body the way it is.

I do my very best every day.

I am constantly learning and growing in my own unique way.

I am patient and I never give up.

I believe in myself and in my inner strength.

I make a masterpiece out of every day.

I deserve respect, kindness, and inclusion.

I am brave and courageous and face all challenges.

I am filled with creativity and unique ideas.

I listen to my heart. My heart knows best what is right and what is wrong.

My life is wonderful.

I am a source of inspiration for others.

I deserve compassion and understanding.

I am happy.

I am beautiful and valuable, inside and out.

I can shed light into the darkness, because the sun is always with me.

I feel safe and secure.

I can speak for those who cannot speak for themselves.

I can change my life if I want to.

I love myself the way I am.

I am unique. I am strong. I can do anything. This inspirational book of motivational affirmations is designed to remind children with disabilities of everything they love about themselves, how powerful they are and that they have unlimited potential.

Daily spoken, these affirmations make them confident, strong, motivated and empathetic. They show these children that they are unique and that they have a lot to offer to the world. A book that teaches them to believe in themselves and to overcome fears. And that shows that every single child is exceptional, has special abilities and can fulfill their dreams.